I WAS NOT MEANT

to

Break

MAGGIE JOHNSON

authorHOUSE®

AuthorHouse™ UK
1663 Liberty Drive
Bloomington, IN 47403 USA
www.authorhouse.co.uk
Phone: UK TFN: 0800 0148641 (Toll Free inside the UK)
*   UK Local: 02036 956322 (+44 20 3695 6322 from outside the UK)*

Published by AuthorHouse 05/13/2021

ISBN: 978-1-6655-8943-7 (sc)
ISBN: 978-1-6655-8942-0 (e)

Print information available on the last page.

Contents

A Tale About a Family

Once upon a time
There was a family.
Consisting of a mum,
A dad, two daughters,
And two sons.

The oldest was eighteen,
The parents' pride and joy.
Until the triplets joined the family,
And everything changed.

What You Taught Me

I've always been about family.
That's what you installed in me
From a young age.
You said families help each other out,
That they are the people
Who will always have your back.

We would spend the spring
At the park with
Grandma, Grandad,
Aunt Anne, Uncle Luke,
Masie, and Dad.

My friends would tell me
They wanted a family like
Ours.

A family always stays together.
That's what you would say to me.
So, what happened to me and you?

An Older Sister

Sometimes I love my job.
I love being an older sister.

Sometimes I hate it.
I hate it when they rely on me.

Trees in Bloom

You used to love this time of year.
The trees are starting to bloom.
The birds are in the sky.
The bees are collecting the pollen.
And our eyes will start to weep.

This is the time for new beginnings,
The time for spring cleaning,
The time to leave the doors open,
A time to eat in the garden.

We won't be doing that this year.
You are on one of your business trips.
But I promise I will send you a picture
Of the trees in bloom.

Bubbles

I got the kids bubbles
In town to take round Grandad's.
They had been so good all week,
They deserved a treat.

I didn't expect much out of them.
When we got to Grandad's,
They asked me for the bubbles,
And into the garden they went
With the dog right behind them,
Ready to catch every bubble
They sent her way.

Easter Outfits

Grandma wanted to take
A photo of her grandchildren
In our easter outfits,
A tradition that started when
Masie and I were born.

The triplets were not into it
Until I told them they could
Have Easter treats
When we were done.

Easter Baskets

I wanted to make all three kids an Easter basket,
Just like the ones you made me when I was their age.

Mine had to be pink.
It would be sitting on the dining room table,
Waiting for me to open.
Colouring books, dot to dots,
Reading books, a toy rabbit, and a headband.
Every year was the same
But exciting, nevertheless.

For the triplets I had to make sure I
had the same of everything
As not to cause an argument.

I hope this will be a tradition they
look forward to every year.

Family Events

It's hard going to family events without you.
People ask me where you are.
Do I lie or tell the truth?
That your business meetings are more important to you
Then spending time with me.
I really don't know what to say anymore.

Rainboots

Samuel wanted his
Rainboots on.
He wanted to splash through
The puddles.
They were only little,
But still he got muddy.
Why did I take him
To the corner shop?
We only needed milk.

Trip

We went on a little
Trip today,
Just me, Dad, and the triplets.

We went to the beach,
Spent our pennies
At the penny slot machines,
Bought ice creams and doughnuts,
And went on a drive through
The back roads with the
Windows down.

Bike Ride

Masie thought it would
Be a good idea to take
The triplets on a bike ride
Round the cul-de-sac.

We got through it with
No scrapes or bruises.
What good luck.

New Flowers

There are two new flowers
In the garden.
The kids have been outside
Every day to watch them grow.
I think Dad was right
To build them a flower bed.
They are so interested in them, Mum.
I hope you are too.

Daffodils

Samuel wanted to
Buy some flowers
To put on the dinner table.

He decided on daffodils
Because they are your favourite.
You should have seen his smile
When the cashier asked him who
The flowers were for.
He proudly said they were for his Mum.

As soon as we got home,
He put the daffodils in a vase,
Ready and waiting for you to get home.

These Small Hours

I love it when Samuel
Asks me to cuddle with him.
He seldom does, so when
He does, I hold on tight,
Scared to let him go.

One day he will grow up,
Not wanting his big sister around,
Not wanting me to embarrass him in front of his friends.

He will ask me not to talk to him
When he is with them.
I will still do it
And laugh when his cheeks grow red.

But for now, he is only four years old.
I have years before he gets to that age.
And when he does, I will remember this moment
Where he is content with his big sister cuddling him.

Decorating Easter Eggs

I decided to make Easter eggs
Out of cardboard
For the kids to paint.

We are going to put them outside
To let the Easter Bunny know:
Please stop here.

Easter Chocolate

Why did the whole
Family have to give
The kids chocolate?

They have been bouncing
Off the walls for hours,
And it's bedtime.

Next year I'm telling
The family to give
The triplets a toy.
That must be better
Than a sugar rush.

Kites Flying

There were hundreds in the sky.
There were no clouds,
And a gentle breeze.
A perfect day to fly a kite.

It would have been so easy
To go to the shops and buy one.
However, you were on your
Way home, and I had to start dinner.

I told the kids we could
All go next weekend
With Grandma and Grandad too.

Numb

I feel numb when I see you.

Should I say hi?
Should I hug you?
Should I tell you my secrets?

You are my mum.
This should come so easy,
But it doesn't.

You never hugged me,
Told me you loved me,
Or read me a bedtime story.
That was Dad's job.

I do it for the triplets,
So they never have to feel
The same way I do when
I look at you.

Mother's Day

—❀—

We were able to surprise
You for Mother's Day
Which is rare; you wake
Up so early most days.

It was the kids' idea
To make breakfast in bed.
I had to wake up extra
Early so the kids could
Write their names in the
Card they made.

I hope you had a wonderful
Mother's Day, Mum.
And yes, even if I
Don't say it to you
Often, I do appreciate
What little you do.

Picnic in the Park

I asked you if you wanted to go to the park
With me and the kids.
You said no, you were too busy to go.

It was a lovely day.
The sun was high in the sky,
Beating down hot rays onto
Our pale skins.
Maybe one day I will get tanned
And not burned.

They were going crazy.
They hadn't been out for days.
They had so much energy
For one person to take.

I phoned Masie on the way.
She was standing outside
The garden gate with a big umbrella
And a picnic basket.

We used to have picnics in the park,
Just me and you,
At least once a week
Whenever the sun was shining.

Now I carry on the tradition
With my cousin and siblings,
Running around the park.

MAGGIE JOHNSON

The Cabin

I have never seen the kids more excited
Than when they saw the cabin for the
First time.

This is where we will be staying
For the next seven days
As a whole family—
Grandma, Grandad, Aunt Anne,
Uncle Luke, and Masie too.

I get out of the car to take
My bags from the boot,
Seeing kids playing
On their bikes.
It's a beautiful day to do so.
I do hope the triplets will
Think so too.

Heartbreak

You never tuck the triplets
into bed.
You did tonight.

I saw you in Holly's room,
Sitting at the edge of the bed
With one hand on hers.

She was asking
Why you had to leave.
You told her you had work.
She would have to stay here
At the cabin
With the rest of the family.

I saw the smile fade
From her lips.
Holly's lips started
To quiver.
I wanted to walk in
And take her in my arms
To tell her everything
Would be okay.

Home Sweet Home

I don't think I will
Ever get tired of home.

It's the place I am my
Most comfortable.
Where I feel loved.
Where laughter happens
Every day.

Why would I want to leave that?

Amsterdam

You knew I was looking
Forward to that trip.
You didn't want me to go.
I stayed behind to help
You with the triplets.

The hardest thing about it?
I had to go with Grandad
To take my friends to the airport.

I had to sit in the front,
Hearing how excited they were,
Knowing that was meant to be me too.

Crying

I'm overwhelmed.
You want me.
Dad wants me.
Grandma wants me.
Grandad wants me.
The triplets want me.

So yes, I do
Break down.
What else am I
Meant to do?

Smile on Your Face

For the first time in a long time
I saw a smile on your face.
It was a strange but beautiful
Thing to see.
You should smile more.
It suits you, Mum.

MAGGIE JOHNSON

Excuse after Excuse

I have heard
The same excuse
A thousand times.

Mum, it gets tiring.
I wish you could
Just say you didn't
Want to pick the triplets
Up; that would have been fine.

Excuse after excuse
Gets boring and annoying.
I wish you could just tell the truth,
And that would be it.

You Don't Care

You don't care that
I'm struggling to keep
My relationships together.

Struggling to keep a routine
For the triplets.

Struggling to put food on the table.

Grandma tries to help me.
I don't want to rely on her.

You don't care about that, do you?

A Choice to Make

—✿—

You can change the plans
With me,
But not with the kids.

I am old enough for it not to bother me.
The kids are a different story.
They ask why you let them down.
What am I meant to say to that, Mum?

Yes, after a while they forget and move on.
But that does not mean you are let off the hook.

You have a choice to make, Mum.
Keep your promises or
See their hearts break.

I Cannot Forget

The ways you shouted at me
For going to the party,
Like it was my duty
To put the kids to bed,
To be home, waiting for you,
Is something I can never forget.

Role Model

I want to be a role model
To the triplets like you
Were to me.

I want to teach them
To be polite,
To say their pleases and
Thank yous,
And to always share
Their things.

It's what you taught me.
I want to teach those
Lessons to them.

I Could Not

I always wanted to make
Everyone happy, but then
I realised I could not.
I am only one person after all.

Pictures

I can picture a time
When we would
All sit down at the table
At six o'clock.
Now it's just the kids and I.
What does that say about us?

Through the Window

If you looked through the window
You would think we were a
Normal family.

We have both parents
Under one roof.
We have a family game night,
And sometimes you will read
A story to the triplets.

What you never see are the hard times,
When the kids are screaming,
When I am crying,
When you come home late.

Everything looks better
When you look through
The window.

Pass Me By

People will walk
In and out of our lives.
That's just life.

That's what you
Told me when
My friend and I
Had arguments.

People will pass,
And new ones will
Come along.

Some will only stay
For a while.
Some will stay
For life.

You never know
Who those people are.
That's the beauty of life.

Hair

I would tell my friends
How you would sit me
Down and play with my
Hair for hours.
Plaits, ponytails, buns—
You did it all.

I didn't realise how difficult it was.
Hannah would not sit still.
I pulled her hair apparently.
In the end I gave up.
I wish you could teach me,
So I can get it right.

Won't Be Little for Long

They won't be little for long,
So put them in wellie boots.
Let them get muddy.
Let them ruin their clothes.
Let them splash in every puddle,
Even if you don't find it funny.

One day they will grow up
And outgrow the cuddles.
Keep them as little as possible,
Before it all goes away.

Balcony

I love sitting on the balcony at night.
It's the only place the triplets
Do not go.
The one place I can just
Relax and unwind.

I like seeing the city lights
Twinkling like stars.
The peace that comes with it
As people are going home
After a long and stressful day
Is my favourite thing
About being on the balcony.

Count Every Moment

I love it when we
All get together.
I love it when we
Can sit down as a
Whole family,
Not just me, Dad,
and the triplets.

Umbrellas

The triplets were fighting
Over the umbrella today.
It wasn't even raining that much.
They wanted to hold it at the same time.
I will never make that mistake again.

Coffee

I wish I could take you
To a coffee shop.
I wish we could talk
And have an honest
Conversation.

We never do anything,
Just the two of us.
Maybe we should
And make it a monthly thing.

It's just a thought.

A Treat

Strawberries and cream were a treat
when Grandad came round.
It was the only dessert he would have after dinner.

One day he put sugar on the strawberries
and put in extra cream just for me.

'Never tell your mother; she will go insane.'
And I never did.

All We Want

I'm right here.
Please don't forget me.
Please don't forget them.
All we want is
Our mum to be
Home with us.

A Home

Can a home still be
A home even when
You are not here?

I Don't Hate You

I never want you to think
I hate you, Mum.
I just get frustrated.
I will never say this to your face
Because when we are good,
We are very good,
And it's almost like you were never
Gone at all.
Why would I want to mess that up?

Just Like Old Times

We went out on a
Mother-daughter day
With Grandma, Aunt Anne, and
Masie.

It was the first time in a long time
I got to spend the whole day
With you
Without the triplets.

It was like I got my old mum back,
The one who used to
Take me clothes shopping,
Take me to go get a coffee,
And buy me something to eat
At my favourite restaurant.

No matter what happens
Tomorrow, I will always look
Back on today as the day
I got my mum back.

That will be enough for me.

To Be with Them

They saw the fireworks
Coming from the neighbour's garden.
They ran out before we could say no.

You didn't want to go.
You wanted to stay inside.
You said you'd watch from the window.

Fireworks scare me.
You know that.
Still I went out with them,
Putting my fears to one side.

Barefoot

Walking barefoot
In the grass
Is the nicest feeling
I have felt in months.

Blue Skies

My whole mood changes
As soon as I see blue skies.

I can let the kids go out.
I can take photos of the
Plants I see on our walks.

I can finally put on the sunglasses
I put away last autumn.

I wish you were back from
Your business trip, Mum.
I managed to get Dad to
Join us on the walk.
I got a nice family photo.
The only person missing
Was you.

Planting Seeds

We went to the garden centre
To get some seeds
To plant in the planter
Dad made last week.

He's hoping the triplets
Will get into gardening.
I'm not so sure.
They say they like something,
But that can change by next week.

I wish you were here.
I wish we could say we
Did this as a family.
But I cannot.

Our Safe Haven

They tell you families are there to support you.
A haven from the trials and tribulations.
A place to settle your burdens.
A sanctuary to hide inside.
Somewhere you can rest without worry
And remember how to breathe.
Why are you not there for me?

They Never Ask

I love my friends.
No matter what happens
Between you and me,
How sad
Or angry
Or bitter I seem,
They never ask.

They walk me into their houses,
Wrap me up in blankets,
And play movies with popcorn for tea,
Until I'm ready to go back
Home again.

Someone's Arms

I fake a smile
Every single time
We have
An argument.
It's better than crying
In someone's arms.

Hindsight

It's such a wonderful thing.
I just wish it would have
Told me all the responsibilities
That I would have.

And how little time
I'd have left
To just be me.

Chances

How many more chances
Can I give you
Before I run out?

If I tell you
This is your last chance
Will anything change?

I've lost count
Of the number of chances
I've given you.

I just know it's more
Than anyone would ever
Give me.

Will You Still Love Me?

If I decided to spread
My wings and fly
High above the clouds
To somewhere far, far away,
Where I can make my own roost
Just for me,
Will you still love me?

Scream

I can scream and shout
Until I'm down to my
Last breath.

But what good
Would that do?
It never makes me feel
Any better.

It only makes things worse.

Raindrops

Raindrops are like
The tears I cry.
They fall on my cheek
And get soaked up
In my skin
Before you even notice
Because there is weakness
In your eyes.

Listen

I just want you
To listen to me.
I need someone
To talk to.

About my worries,
My mistakes,
My hopes,
My dreams,
My achievements.

But there is no one.
So I write them down
Like a poem
No one will read.

Keeping It Together

You can run when the kids
Get too much.
You can cry when work
Gets on top of you.
You can lock the door of your bedroom,
Because we know we can't come in
If the doors are locked.

You can do all those things
And get away with it.
But when it's my turn,
I simply cannot.

Someone needs to be strong.
Someone needs to keep this
Family together.
That someone is me.

Because you won't do it,
Will you?

What a Smile Can Hide

A smile can hide a lot.
It can hide embarrassment.
It can hide pain.
It can also hide something nice,
Like a laugh just bursting to come out.

My smile, what does it hide?
Disappointment.
My smile hides the disappointment
That you won't be home in time for my birthday.
That's what a smile can hide.

I Miss Her

I miss her, Mum.
I miss her, and she hasn't even left.

Masie goes back to uni in
Two days,
Leaving me to do
The school drop-offs
And pick-ups
On my own.

I wish she could have stayed longer.
I wish we could have gone somewhere,
Just the two of us.
Some things are just not meant to be.

Already I miss
All the things
We could have done.

Case of the Mondays

I hate Mondays.
Everyone says it's the start
Of a brand-new week,
But I see it as a fight:
To get the triplets to school.
To get the shopping for the week.
To spend time with my friends.
To find the motivation
To carry on
Just one more week
Until you're home again.

Sixteen

I can do things
On my own.
I've been doing them
Since I was sixteen.

I have looked after
The triplets
On my own.
I've fed them,
Stayed up with them,
And taken them to school
On my own.

I have done everything
You ever wanted me to.
Now I need to do the things
I have always wanted to.

Today,
I'll do all those things
On my own.

A Thousand Times

I have built a high wall
From my head to my toes
To protect my heart from hurt.
I'm scared it will break.

I don't want people
To tell me what to feel.
I don't want people
To get too close.

Because that's when I'm
In danger the most
Of that high wall
Crumbling into

A thousand tiny pieces
From my head to my toes
To pierce my heart.
I'm scared it will
Hurt.

Will I Ever?

Will I ever
Be able to let
You go?

Will I ever
Be able to say
I don't need
Your approval?

Will I ever
Be able to make
You proud?

Will I ever
Be able to get
That special relationship with you
Back?

Will I ever?

I just don't know.

I Lie

I lie to the triplets
To keep them happy.

I lie to Grandma
To pretend I'm okay.

I lie to Grandad
To stop him from worrying.

I lie to Dad
To feel better about missing out.

I lie to Masie
About being content where I am.

I lie to you,
Telling you I don't mind you being away.

And I lie to myself,
Saying that I'm not lying at all.

That it doesn't hurt.
That I don't feel alone.

I've never been
A very good liar.

So when did I start
Telling so many lies?

Put on a Show

We always put on a show
When others are around.
We pretend we didn't
Just have a screaming match
In the car,
Or that we haven't been
Speaking to each other
For two days.
It's just easier to let others
Think everything is all right
And move on.

By My Bedside

I have a photo of us
By my bedside
That I look at
When you aren't here.

I look at it when I need
To talk to you,
But don't know what to say.

I hide it under my pillow
When you come in,
Replacing it with a photo
Of me and the triplets.

As if having a photo
Of me and my Mum
Is something
To be ashamed of.

My Fears

I thought when I left school
All my fears would shrink.

That they'd get smaller
And smaller
And smaller
And one day, they'd be so
Small
I wouldn't be able to see them anymore.

Instead,
My fears grew
Ten times more.

The fear of
Letting you down.

The fear of
Not getting the triplets
To school on time.

The fear that I would
Be on my own
With no one to help me.

MAGGIE JOHNSON

Bigger
And bigger
And bigger
And now they're so
Big
I can't see anything else.

Friends Worth Having

My friends are there for me
No matter what.
I phone them at silly times
To tell them all my problems.
They always tell me what to do,
And always make me see your
Point of view.

I feel sad because I don't
Do the same for them.
They tell me I have enough
On my plate;
I don't need to deal with
Their problems too.

Still, I feel guilty.
They don't let me feel
Guilty for long.

Those are the friends
Everyone should have.

MAGGIE JOHNSON

The Good Times

The good times are the times
We have spent as a family.
When you would turn off your phone,
Put your work away,
And we would go out for the day.

Nothing would distract you
And with extra eyes and hands
To keep the triplets out of trouble
I could enjoy every moment
Being with you.

The last time we did this
We went to the teahouse
With Grandma and Grandad.
You spent the whole
Time laughing.
It was the best day ever.

What I Would Tell You

What would I do
If you were here
For a few moments more?

I would sit you down and
Show you my exam results.
You would be so happy.
I got an A+.

You would phone Grandma,
Arrange a meal to celebrate,
And ask me what I want to do
In the future.

But you did none of that.
You looked away before
I even got the chance
To hand over the envelope.
Thanks a lot, Mum.

Second Chances

I believe in giving people
Second chances.

What I don't believe
Is when you give someone
A second chance,

And they throw it
Back in your face.

Pretend

How can you pretend
Not to care
When you so badly do?

Even Though

Even though I don't say it,
I still love you.

What's Said and Done

I have said everything
I wanted to say to you,
And you have said everything
You wanted to say to me.

But even with our voices raised
And our emotions let loose
'Everything' isn't enough
For either of us to be heard.

We could do this again
And again
And again
And nothing would change.

So let's just move on from it.
Let it just be said and done.

My Tender Heart

I've learnt how to
Protect my tender heart from
Being broken.
When my walls aren't
High enough
Or strong enough
And it's left exposed
Beating painfully
In my chest.

It's a simple fix
And it works so well.

I never hand it out.

Suffering

I can deal with you not being here.
I've dealt with it for so long,
It doesn't hurt anymore.

Except for the moments
When I'm scared
And alone
And overwhelmed
Which happen more and more
The longer you're away.

I can deal with the stress
And the hurt
And the pain.
It doesn't bother me anymore.

But *they* are suffering with you
Being away.

To Myself

I tend to keep
How I'm feeling
To myself.
Locked up tight
Behind my ribs
Next to my heart.
I never want
To be a burden
To anyone.

Text

I got a text from a friend
Telling me we can't meet up.
I should be used to disappointment.
I should be used to plans changing.
I still have that crushed feeling
Every single time I see,
'I'm sorry.'

On a Loop

I hate it when all the
Good times we have
Are only there
In my memory,
Playing on a loop
Like a carousel.
Each horse a memory
To remind me of
The relationship
We once had.

People All Around

I have been staring at the
Blank screen for two hours,
Sitting in Grandad's chair
To feel closer to him.

Today was his funeral.
It was the last time I will
Ever get to see him,
Sleeping soundly
In his forever bed.

There are people all around
Celebrating his life.
I should be thanking everyone
For coming, but I can't.
I don't even want to move.

He was my life.
Now all that's left of the man
Who took me out to castles
And fetes and forests and fairs
Is his chair.

Live with Me

I have had an offer
To go and live with Teresa
And Roseanna.
The three of us under
One roof
With no one else.
I'm going to take it.

It's what Grandad would
Have wanted.

It's what I want.

Risk Another Goodbye

I cannot risk
Another goodbye.
I have already
Lost too much.
Please
Don't let this be
Another ending.

Rainbow

I saw a rainbow
In the sky.
I told the kids
It was Grandad
Saying hi.

A New Life

I need to start thinking about me.
That's all Grandad ever wanted.
I just didn't notice.

I need to start going out with my friends
And stop giving in to you, Mum.
There will be a time when I won't be
Living at home.
Maybe I'll even have a family of my own.

I won't always be there to look after the kids.
You need to start doing it on your own, Mum.
I have a life that is calling my name.
I want to catch it before it goes away.

There's a Silver Lining

It's been two months
Since Grandad passed away,
And there has been a big change.

You cut down on work travel
To spend time with the triplets.

You take them to school,
Pick them up,
Make the dinners at night,
And tuck them into bed
While singing lullabies.

You switch off your phone,
Put your laptop to one side,
File your paperwork away,
And go out on long walks.

Two triplets in your arms
And one in Dad's
For a photo that sits above
The fireplace
Where everyone is
Smiling.

Grandma is now living with us
After weeks persuasion,
Seeing more of her daughter
Than she has in years.

And for the very first time
I have spread my wings,
Soaring high above the clouds;
I am going to university
With Masie and my friends.

This is everything
Grandad would have wanted.

Printed in Great Britain
by Amazon